Soar On Purpose

Soar On Purpose

Ann Marie Bolton

Library of Congress Control Number:		2020911005
ISBN:	Hardcover	978-1-9845-8373-4
	Softcover	978-1-9845-8372-7
	eBook	978-1-9845-8371-0

Print information available on the last page.

Rev. date: 07/28/2020

To order additional copies of this book, contact:
Xlibris
1-888-795-4274
www.Xlibris.com
Orders@Xlibris.com
814996

Contents

Please use this book as a success manual. Share it with friends, let's all succeed together.

Introduction

Ann Marie Smith-Bolton born and grew up in Cameron, nestled in Westmoreland, Jamaica West Indies. Traumatized by happenings in the earlier years of her life has led her to share with everyone who need a boost of energy to let them realize that setbacks are a sure sign of a positive victorious comebacks but you must be persistent and persevere, with the right mental attitude. I have an innate ability to charm. Expecting the best for my life and others. I am an encourager. I look to God only for validation. I am a child of God and I am approved by God. As a kingdom citizen, I am handpicked by God and He has placed seeds of greatness in my life. I am a masterpiece of the Creator. Thank God I am living under an open heaven only because of the supernatural favour of God on my life.

Ann Marie Smith-Bolton is a Philanthropist, who wear many hats. She believes in the anointing and full immersion of the Holy Spirit. Fasting, praise and worship is my lifestyle, that's where I find strength and build my spiritual muscles. I seek daily to impact people's lives, adding value to everyone I come in contact with. Out of my passion for helping others and being a Philanthropist. I founded an association in my community, geared towards assisting and empowering the youths and community at large.

As the Founder and President of the New Galloway Citizens Association, I assisted youths with bursaries and back to school supplies. I operate a free employment agency where some of the parents and the youths gained, gainful employment. These are the things I find fulfilment in assisting others and by the grace of God I will continue touching lives positively.

This book is a beautiful and inspirational story, decorated with life experiences that will empower you and change your lives forever. Its aim is to empower, raise up eagles and will enhance and positively transform your lives, failing your way to success. **HOLD YOUR HEADS UP!** Encourage yourself! Do not bury great ideas in our mental grave yard. Build a solid foundation these are building blocks for your future, unshakable we are. Come let's journey together, you will be empowered and inspired. You will never be the same. Be reminded that **FORGIVENESS** is the vital ingredient on the journey.

ANN MARIE SMITH-BOLTON

Acknowledgement

I pen these lines on the promise and premise of God my Rock, my Sword, my Shield, my Strength, my Strong Tower, my Hiding Place, my Deliverer, my Healer, my Waymaker, my Light in the darkness and a faithful Father, just to name a few of the many Names of God.

With a grateful heart, I extend my gratitude and appreciation to the following beacons of my life:

My Parents, the Late George and Sylvia Smith – Thanks for molding and instilling values and attitude in us and teaching us to become the true winners, overcomers and Leaders we are today. Your legacy will forever live on forever.

My sons, Ricardo and Rhori Bolton – I am truly humbled to be your mother and to have you as my sons. We share a knitted relationship with love and respect for each other. You both are the best and I love and appreciate you. Thank you for believing in me and trusting me. With God's divine intervention, I have nurtured you and instilled godly principles in you both that will carry you throughout the rest of your lives.

You both stood with me through all of life's challenges. Thank God we can now look back and realize that all our challenges are turned into golden opportunities and enhanced spiritual growth. I thank God for you both. My family means everything to me. Thanks to the persons who have helped me through difficult challenges. It is through these challenging encounters that I am molded into who I am today. Thank you. Thanks to all who saw the good in me and encouraged me on my journey, thanks for your prayerful support.

Deenie E. Craig-Bolton and the Late Albert Bolton – What great legacy you have imparted to us as a family. Your lives and ministry have truly molded us, as you carefully modeled the life of who a true believer should be and for this, I am forever grateful. A life well lived for Christ.

My siblings – Thanks to Carol, the late Fitzgerald, Carl, Charmaine and Cosland you all hold a place so dear in my heart. May God continually bless you all and your families.

It would be remiss not to mention my former husband of Twenty Two (22) years and the father of my two sons. Reflecting on the years spent together, he was a confidante, a friend and a good father. He has given us a solid foundation as a family to continue to build on. May the Lord continue to bless him in all his future endeavours.

"Let us be grateful to the people who make us happy; they are the charming gardeners who make our souls blossom.
- Marcel Proust

Chapter One

Be Prepared for Speed Humps

It was a beautiful Thursday in May when I gracefully entered this world, orchestrated by the love of my Creator, born to Sylvia Smith (deceased) and George Smith (deceased). The fourth of five siblings, I was truly another bundle of joy who came into their lives. As a parent myself, I can imagine another child coming into their lives: how happy they were. My dad travelled to almost every parish on work related trips. Growing up my dad and I had a great relationship. My dad was my hero.

My parents were avid believers, knowing they serve a faithful God and He will never let them down, as long as they believe. We lived beside the church for many years. We grew up in the Nazarene church. My dad was a church builder and planter. He went around to different parishes and laid foundations and built churches. My dad being a church builder and church planter, proves to us that our God is a limitless God. We are vessels ready to be used by Him. He is working behind the scene on our behalf, we just have to remove all limitation and put our faith in action and believe, He will do what He said He will do. That's what my parents did when I entered this world.

Parents can only give good advice or put them on the right paths, but the final forming of a person's character lies in their own hands.
- Anne Frank

They believed God and trusted and obeyed the will of God for their lives. God is in control and He will ensure we have good success as believers. My parents they believed

God for the best. We grew up in the church so all the different activities of the church, as children we were involved in. I can remember my sister and I sang at every program held at the church. I started singing publicly since I was eight (8) years old. There was a poem I always recite at these programs, it goes like this "flowers on my shoulders, slippers on my feet, I am mommy's darling don't you think I'm sweet?" That's a poem that garnered and harnessed much confidence in me. Thanks to my parents my first mentors.

My mother left a legacy, she founded the Galloway Basic School which was located beside the Mt. Grace Nazarene church. This school is still operational. I can remember our home, was where all the visiting Pastors ate. My mother was a very hospitable person, she does most of the cooking. She was like a mother to everyone. Sometimes we are eating and someone shows up on our step. My mother would share them a plate of meal, this I really admired. She treats everyone with love, respect and dignity. My dad had the breakfast duties. I can recall us having fried dumplings, my dad was the one who taught me how to use my hand and not the fork to remove the fried dumplings from the frying pan, made some you can relate. We were given the most nutritious meals, our breakfast were mainly consisted of cooked green bananas, liver, porridge, callaloo, ackee and saltfish, etc. My parents were my first role models. They taught us well and were strict in every sense of the word. We were not allowed to go to our neighbours house. We were only allowed in summer holidays to go to our grandma, aunts and uncles house, in Cambridge, St. James for summer holidays. This we anticipated each summer. Most times when we return home though we were sick, this was the only drawback, but others wise it was fun. This brings back fond memories.

They did not allow us to go anywhere except for church. I can recall when I was to go recite a poem at a festival my mom said no. My teacher said I had to go to represent my school. That day in particular, I wore one of my regular (old) uniforms, had my mom known, she would have given me a newer uniform to wear. My teacher took me to represent my school and we won. Congratulations! Just to show you how strict my mom was. It was my teacher who had to make the decision for me to go represent my school. All of this was Divine.

With every Divine promise there is a perfect timing. I can also remember as a child, my neighbours were farmers. One of their crops was rice, when it was time to reap the rice, they would stay up late at nights and separate the trash from the rice itself. This process was quite interesting. They would put them on the ground and go around in a circle and beat the trash with sticks until the rice is separated. This was quite entertaining because they sung a song while labouring. As children we were not allowed to go over there but we could hear them from our home it was really fun. Trusting God's timing is everything. As we got bigger we were able to do things were not able to do as a child, was is understandable. We stayed the course. When God makes a promise to us, it is imperative that we are prayerful about this promise. We often try to assist God and when we do we tamper with the result because we are impatient. We must wait on God, scripture tells us:

But they that wait upon the Lord shall renew their strength; they shall mount up, with wings as eagles; they shall run, and not be weary and they shall walk and not faint. (Isaiah 40:31 KJV)

I believe I was a promised child to my parents. When we wait on the Lord. He gives us strength and endurance. It is impossible to do it in our own strength. God is faithful and He will not let us down. My mother worked as a Household Helper to Teacher Brown and she also sells at Coke's View Primary School, just a stone throw away from home, my dad was a mason. My mother (Ms. Sylvie) was known for her kindness to the students at the school because whether or not they had the money to purchase a snack, they were going to get what they needed. Her kindness echoed in the community to date. These are seeds she has sown and left a legacy that will forever live on.

"Your children need your presence more than your presents"
-Jesse Jackson

This day in particular, both my parents went to work and left us with the nanny and then a freak accident took place at my home. This is what I was told by my parents. My nanny was frying fish and I was on the verandah playing, the pot over heated when she placed the fish in the frying pan and the frying pan caught fire. Imagine that for a moment, she panicked took the frying pan off the stove instead of going through the kitchen door, she came towards the verandah where I was playing and she flung the pot away and sadly, she accidentally threw it on me. I can imagine how horrible she felt.

People said it was deliberately done, this I cannot agree with, no one I believe would be so heartless to hurt or harm an innocent child. I received third degree burns to my entire body. My head, my face my arms, all over my body I received third degree burns. I was severely burnt and given over to die (oh my God). I cannot to date fathom how gruesome and painful this must have been to a baby just Eighteen (18) months old.

I was severely burned and received third degree burns to my entire body, to date this is a miracle most of my scars have all disappeared. Thank God the same way God was in the fire with the Three Hebrew boys, He was in the fire with me protecting me. My scars are at places they were meant to be. My parents were told by the doctor that I was going to die.

My parents are God fearing and never believed that lie from the devil. They prayed and prayed and called on other prayer warriors and elders of the church for help and they undergirded them in prayer and thanks be to God I recovered miraculously. I received third degree burns to my entire body nowhere was spared but most scars have miraculously disappeared. **Now my scars are my stars**.

I boldly share and encourage others who have been marred or experienced some form of setback or tragedy that they can make a difference in spite of scars. **Scars are our trophy to show us we fought and we won**. I spent one year in the hospital and was discharged in December for my Christmas gift and a present to my family as well. I am sure that was the best present they were anticipating that year. I can imagine what my parents and older siblings went through because they had to nurse my wounds. I was told that I scratched my head so bad, that blood was always in my finger nails. That was gruesome and uncomfortable for a child. I can just imagine. Thank you Lord.

I forgave my nanny, walking around with anger, bitterness and unforgiveness affects no one but us, it only poison our future, this I would never allow, contaminating my life is certainly something I would not do. Let go the negatives of your past and be set free, no baggage thank God.

When I started going to school because I had lost some of my hair on my head. My mom parted my hair in five plaits. Three to the front and two to the back, two ribbons were always tied to the two back plaits. The ribbons at the back was used to hide the areas with no hair, my mom would use hair pins to hold the ribbon in place so when the wind blows it would not show the bald areas caused by the burn (accident I had at home).

As unfortunate as it was, every different stage of my life, there was a solution to hide my scars. I can recall when I was going to Unity Primary School, my brother Cosland

and I attended the same school. At the time my mom was working at Paradise Supermarket as a cashier. This she did for over Twenty (20) years. In the evenings after school dismissed. We would normally wait on my mother at the school gate. At that time there was a big bus known as rubies that my mom takes to go home. She would stop and called out for us and they would push us through the window because the bus was too pack. I am petite in size to date, I am 5'1' so it was easy for me to go through the window. Those were the days. God is truly awesome.

When I grew older and started attending High school my mom braided my hair, which was a great style to mask my scars or baldness. When I left High School extensions were in style so that was an opportunity to upgrade and enhance my appearance. My hairdressers and Jacqueline Smith from Savanna-La-Mar, Westmoreland and Jacqueline Fogo from Montego Bay, Jamaica they are the best.

They were so tender to my hair and most importantly they understood that I lost some of my hair and I would not want anyone else in the shop to see my baldness. They would take care of my hair in the back of the shop so as to keep my scars hidden. This I appreciate and thank them from the bottom of my heart. I also found the different styles of wigs are a true blessing. Wigs I thought I would never wear but trying one was all I needed. I am wearing extensions and wigs to date. How great our God is, in every situation, He makes away. I am forever grateful to the Almighty God.

"When we believe, trust, and take direction from the perspective that our setbacks are in fact setups for success, then it increases the likelihood of future victories"
- Charles F Glassman

My mother was my first seamstress, she would sew our clothes both for church and work. My mother was the best mom. May her sweet soul rest in peace. Our parents left us a legacy. It is important that we tune our spiritual frequency to the Holy Spirit, He will Divinely connect to us by Faith. In doing so, the flesh must be sacrificed, we must kill the flesh and trust God for the best. My parents trusted God for everything. We grew up in the Nazarene Church and we lived beside the church. We were taught that Christ is the only way and thank God to date He is still the only way and will always be. As soon as the church doors are open we were there. We never missed a service that was how we were brought up as God-fearing children.

My dad was a Lay Preacher/Deacon and he did his job well. We then moved away from beside the church some years later and we lived some miles away from the church. We attended the same church and we never missed a service. My dad, at the time had a motorcycle and he would carry my mother to church on the motorcycle, while we had to run behind them, so we all got to church together and on time.

"When we are children we seldom think of the future. This innocence leaves us

free to enjoy ourselves as few adults can. The day we fret about the future is the day we leave our childhood behind".
- Patrick Rothfuss

One may think that was very hard but as children we too were committed to the church, to even think like that. This was easy to do and it was fun. Life can be pretty challenging but come with me on this journey and let us change our **challenges into opportunities of Happiness. No matter what you are going through or have faced, you are reminded that there is hope.**

I had a situation in my life which I prayed and prayed about and what I wanted to see happened or change, it never did. As I said 'I' but the mistake I made was I never consulted God to ascertain if this was what He wanted for my life. At the time, the flesh was too dominant, so I was left disappointed. Thank God I can now look back and rejoice for the lessons it has taught me. Everything that we encounter, a challenge as difficult as it is, there is a life lesson to be learnt, we must pay attention. The promise must come to pass and with the correct attitude it will. I seek opportunity and not security and in Christ I find peace.

For I know the thoughts that I think toward you, saith the Lord, thoughts of peace, and not of evil, to give you an expected end. Jeremiah 29:11 KJV

Notes

NOTES

1

I Am With You

Scripture: Matthew 28:20

Teaching them to observe all things whatsoever I have commanded you: and, lo, I am with you always, (even) unto the end of the world. Amen.

Start your day with a bang. What is a bang? It is starting your day with prayers and a few moments in the presence of the Holy One who is Jesus Christ. A positive thought and motivational thoughts are also helpful tools to start off your day but when we give the first part of our day to God rest assured you will have a successful day. As the scriptures says, God has promised He will never leave us or forsake us. God is a promise keeper and He is a faithful God.

Prayer: Father in Heaven, thank you for a new day and for giving me the health and strength for my daily tasks. Thank you for loving me in Jesus' Name Amen.

When we make helping others a priority
we sow seeds of greatness.
Ann Marie Bolton

The Lord is on my side; I will not fear Psalm 118:6

Chapter Two

The Key to Happiness

Happiness is solely dependent on oneself. I take great responsibility in ensuring my happiness and the happiness of those whom I come into contact with. I ensure that my encounter with others is a positive and impactful one. I implore you to dwell only on the positives exuding the right energy and attracting the best. The key to happiness is, we must forgive to grow and in this way we maintain our happiness. Serving God and keeping His commandment is what makes us happy.

"The most important thing is to enjoy your life – to be happy – it's all that matters"
-Audrey Hepburn

I have experienced many negative happenings in my personal life but that did not deter my positive perspective on life. It's my perspective that keeps me unstuck. I am sharing my life experience with my readers because a bad break do not have to stop us and make us bitter and angry. Instead, fill our hearts with peace and love, that's where happiness is found. When we invite God into our difficulties He makes away in our difficult situation. Happiness is found only in Jesus Christ. God gives us grace to endure. In every negative or bad situation I found good and lasting life lessons but we must pay attention.

My advice to everyone is, do not look to outside force for happiness: happiness comes from within and you must take responsibility for your happiness. Happiness is contagious. My scars could have caused me to be very unhappy but I choose to be a happy positive camper.

When I started to work and now need to look like an attractive young lady I met my former husband, and he was the one who was now sourcing my extensions and wigs and for this I am grateful. Thank you Fitz, you were always there for me. Can I tell you, this guy could shop. He started travelling overseas and upon his return and he brought back a lot of goodies for his family. After my husband started travelling that's when I noticed changes in our marriage. Later on in this book, my marriage experience will be elaborated on. My marriage brought me closer to God.

We must seek God before we need Him. Seeking God daily will bring about joy, peace and happiness. This peace and joy I have nothing or no one can take it away from you. Be a positive influence and make lasting friendships by being positive. I choose daily to share with others in whatever way I can and by doing so, it gives me great joy and a sense of fulfilment. We are created on purpose for a purpose, so you should not allow anyone or anything to rob you of such legacy. Be happy, God is a faithful God. My scars never stopped me from becoming the giant I am in my faith today. Keep thriving for excellence all you need to have is a persistent spirit.

"Take responsibility of your own happiness, never put it in other people's hands"
- Roy T. Bennett

Choose to help others, even when you need it yourself. Be reminded God is a faithful God. Scars or no scars,

He is the giver of life. He is the Creator and He is the one who determines our happiness. We will be faced with challenging, difficult situations but be happy and turn your worry into worship, come with me on this adventurous beautiful journey. You will be glad you did. Our dreams or our situation can make us feel like we are in a pit and it may feel like there is no way out but God's goodness and mercy is following us. All battles are won in the mind. Positive self-talks are essential in our well being.

The words you use can influence your life.
Positive words are well spring of life.
Lailah Gifty Akita

Turn around those negative thoughts into positive thoughts. God gives us the grace to overcome. God has already given us the victory. We serve a great big wonderful God. Employ that can do attitude. Think yourself to success. Stop committing mental suicide. Fear is a psychological infection. Radiate confidence. Speak up and out. Walk briskly and poised. Your blessings is in your mouth. I communicate well with people at all levels. Action cures fear. Let no one punch holes in your confidence. Withdraw only positive thoughts from your memory bank. Think like a millionaire and it will manifest itself as you work smarter. Have an expanded version of yourself.

Our destiny is decorated with divine favour. God's promises are true. Are you faced with an unbearable situation, employ the right attitude and break those negative cycles. Do not fear anything or anyone except the Lord

God Almighty and honour God with your whole heart. Have power thoughts not negative limiting thoughts and you will be happy. Each circumstance is a teacher to us. Let's enjoy life's journey and spread the love. The future belongs to those who create it.

We have access by faith to fully enjoy our God-given benefits and without hesitation. Each day as we step out in FAITH, God is opening up supernatural doors for us. Decisions of our lives affect our destiny. Happiness is a choice, faith in Jesus Christ keeps peace and joy in our hearts and life. Your personal energy will attract the right people. We have access to eternal life through the Blood of Jesus Christ. Focus on the positive and there you will find peace and happiness. We thank the Lord for the price He paid to redeem us.

When He said it is finished, He meant it. Stop focusing on a negative past. A bad deal or divorce. Stop living life through the rear view mirror. Keep moving forward by FAITH and be happy. When we make the right choices it bring about happiness. Our execution is of utmost importance to our success. Choose wisely and carefully. Our positive choices change the trajectory of our lives. No more lack, no more mediocre living and the list goes on. It is FINISHED. We walk in abundance, we talk abundance and we live in abundance. We are set free from all limitations. Let's keep our eyes on Jesus Christ.

"Everyone enjoys being inspired. But here's the truth when it comes to personal growth; motivation gets you going but discipline keeps you growing'
- John C. Maxwell

God's favour sets us apart from the crowd, we are royalty. Believers walk in Divine favour, authority and power. Trying is not good enough. Doing our best is the correct option. Faith is an action word. We live by faith and not by sight. We are winners both in the natural and in the spiritual. We are on the winning side because we choose to be happy. The enemy has to retreat and he has to surrender to the authority of the Holy Spirit. Rest assured, when you are faced with trials, the favour of God, ward off the enemy. Sometimes the Lord allows our faith to be tested but our tests come to make us better representatives of the gospel of Christ. Our test is our testimony.

"Be a lifter of other people; encourage somebody, bless them, pray with them, trust God for their miracle until it comes."
- John Ndeere

In 1997 I was involved in a motor vehicle accident, at the time I was pregnant with my son. It was critical but thank God, it's only a miracle that saved our lives. When God favors us, He goes ahead remove all obstacles and barriers. One may want to question God, why did He allowed this to happen. God has a plan for each person's life. I was compensated in ways unimaginable for that accident. The motor vehicle accident was a blessing in disguise. Good things are disguised in bad situations.

My son was born a normal child. This is a miracle, to God be the Glory, we are eternally grateful to the Almighty God. Through this experience I gained spiritually because my faith grew and I now believe there is nothing too hard for God to do. As God reveals himself to me more and more He shows me how faithful He is. I serve God with enthusiasm and happiness, what God has done for me, He will do it for you. God is not a partial God, He is fair and just.

"Live your truth. Express your love. Share your enthusiasm. Take action towards your dreams. Walk your talk. Dance and sing to your music. Embrace your blessings. Make today worth remembering".
- Steve Maraboli

God stepped out and pulled me out of the wreckage. He is watching over us and He intervened and saved our lives, thank you Lord. Just imagine for a moment, being pregnant and involved in an automobile accident. Yes it was traumatizing but I was at peace. Everything happen in life for a reason and for a purpose. I was at sweet peace, which comes only from the Holy Spirit. I had no fear because it's faith over fear. Fear cripples, faith gives us wings to soar like eagles. I praised God and thank Him for a great outcome and that's just what happened, amazing God.

"Do not go where the path may lead, go instead where there is no path and leave a trail".
- Ralph Waldo Emerson

We all have access, we must be willing and obedient and be hungry and thirsty. The vehicle was driven by my father-in-law (deceased), he suffered minor injuries along with other occupants. I was the only one who received critical but non-life threatening injuries. The vehicle was mangled, everyone thought the person in the front passenger's seat must be dead. I was the one sitting there, thankfully I am here to tell the tale. It was a truck and a van, head-on collision. At the time of the impact I was singing "I can't even walk without you holding my hand," then I shouted Jesus! The rest is history, only a miracle.

I was taken from the scene of the accident by a taxi driver to the hospital, I believe he is from Bethel Town because the accident happened in Shettlewood, Hanover. While driving he was shouting and tooting his horn "saying save a life, save a life." To date I do not know who this angel was. I would love to meet this person to tell him how grateful I am.

I am nothing but an imperfect being, who is residing on earth with a perfect God as my guidance and protection.
- Edmond Mbiaka

The vehicle was totalled and thank God all lives were saved even my unborn child who is now Twenty Two (22) years old I am indeed grateful to God and all those involved. When God favours you, He protects you. He gives His angels charge over us to keep us in all our ways. Hallelujah! You are protected and guarded by God.

I am here to make a difference to be a participant not a spectator. Do not allow "but" to keep you away from your dream. I never gave up because of the negative circumstances, I stayed the course and is happy with my life, knowing I am pleasing God daily.

Focus on your strengths, not your weaknesses.
Focus on your character, not your reputation.
Focus on your blessing, not your misfortunes.
- Roy T. Bennett

I was on my way home from work when this accident occurred. I was hospitalized for weeks, this was frightening, yet I remained calm. Reminiscing, I can see how favored I truly am walking in His awesome Presence. That same night beside me another lady was admitted in the hospital, she was involved in a motor vehicle accident also. She was placed beside my bed, the nurses worked on her all night but she did not make it through the night, so sad picture.

Days went by and I was still in the hospital. The nurses and doctors could not figure out why I was so happy, considering my circumstances but God was with me and he reminded me that everything was going to be alright and with confidence I released my faith in God and believed.

"Do not underestimate the positive energies you create when you know how to be grateful with daily miracles surrounding you."
- Henry Good

You are reading this book, it is not by coincidence, it is divinely orchestrated by God, for you to purchase this book and I thank you. My readers I prophesy over your lives right now that everything is going to be alright. Your destiny is bright. Keep soaring! The same God that saved me out of that major accident is the same God working in your behalf.

He is working miracles behind the scene for you and me. My advice to you is to seek God before you need him. Look through your minds eyes and know that you are more than able, God is fighting our battles for us. Let nothing stop you from living up to your true potential. You have a lot of untapped resources, don't be afraid to take risks. Will it be easy No, is it possible Yes! You must go through in order for you to be successful. You will have many oppositions in life but do not give up. DO NOT QUIT! Nurture and develop the hunger in you.

Notes

NOTES

2

Make Your Request Known

Scripture: Matthew 7:7

"Ask, and it shall be given."

As we start a new day, ask God for what you need according to the will of God for your lives. Ask God what would He want you to do, today and everyday. We are not on own agenda God is in control of our lives and we must seek His heart and not only His hands.

The scripture says we should ask, ask our Heavenly Father for what He desires for our lives and He will ensure it comes to fruition. He is our Heavenly Father and He is cognizant of what we need for the journey even before we ask.

We may have made requests that are not in alignment with our destiny and because God knows our request may do more harm than good He does not allow it. What a wonderful Father. Rest assured God has our best interest at heart and He is working behind the scene on our behalf.

Prayer: Father in Heaven, as we make our requests please help us to remain in your will for our lives in Jesus' Name Amen.

Aspire for greatness and never give up on your dreams.
-Ann Marie Bolton

CHAPTER THREE

Visible Scars vs Invisible Scars

The little of my visible scars that were left because of my accident caused me much pain in my teenage years. I was ridiculed by my siblings and school mates. I was bullied so badly at school because of my scars, I was afraid to attend school. My parents were not aware of this because I shared it with no one everything was bottled up within me. I did not feel comfortable in discussing this with anyone. It was an extremely painful situation to deal with attending school being fearful, it took its toll on me because in my subconscious it was always there because I was concerned with what is next.

"The wound is the place where the light enter you."
- Rumi

When I should be focused on my studies I was fearful about the children who were causing me much pain and discomfort. I continue to share my experience, my first time sharing was in May 2020, no one knew. I am happy to share and feel more comfortable to share now because I am healed. Healing takes time because it is a process. This did not deter me because children will always be children. I was bullied so bad but never responded and because of that the bullies came at me wanting to get physical, as in fighting me but thankfully a lady intervened and scared them away.

"One's dignity may be assaulted, vandalized and cruelly mocked but it can never be taken away unless it is surrendered"
Michael J. Fox

Bullying is wrong and must be eradicated from our schools and sadly our homes. Thank God I never thought of anything negative, I always maintain a positive mental attitude and that was how I overcame the bullies in my school and environs. I made it up in my mind that God has me here for a purpose which must be fulfilled (Jeremiah 29:11 KJV) I set my goals which later became my vision and I worked smart and hard to accomplish them. I have experienced adversities and unfair treatment but never have I held a pity party. I had a praise party instead I find joy in praising God. God has a purpose for my life which must be fulfilled by His grace. Do not allow injustice to get you down. DREAM BIG!

"Scars have the power to remind us that our past is real"
- Cormac McCarthy

My visible scars have motivated me to be the best that I can be. They have reminded me of the scars in Jesus' hands and feet, they are in His body for you and me. My scars are on my body to positively motivate and inspire my readers that they are unstoppable. Do not allow anything to get into your way, thrive for success and be your best.

I have now come to the conclusion from my personal experiences that scars visible or invisible have nothing to do with one's achievement. I am here to motivate and encourage someone who maybe traumatized by some scars visible or invisible that with the correct mindset you are unstoppable and you will accomplish your goals, just stay focus and have a new perspective. Don't let your dream die! Invite Christ in your circumstances. You are a WINNER! Anything that is trying to stop you is temporary not permanent.

"From every wound there is a scar, and every scar tells a story. A story that says, I survived."
- Craig Scott

You may be faced with a bad report from the doctor, your teenage child is not what you were expecting, you just lost your job, you have a dysfunctional family, your spouse told you he is leaving you for someone else or you may be in debt. I am here to tell you that there is hope. Be prayerful and give thanks even before it manifest itself. Giving God thanks through the process, in advance before its manifestation, is a great act of FAITH.

There are things we have no control over, we just got to do our part and trust God, be confident that He will and is working on your behalf, rest assured He is doing His best. You may have suffered rejection like myself but do not allow that to stop you. That should be seen as a motivation to keep going, it's taking you to the next level in your lives. Life can be treacherous and those negative circumstances helps us to grow.

For there to be betrayal, there would have to have been trust first."
- Suzanne Collin

I am encouraging you from my own personal experience; after Twenty Two (22) years of marriage, I was betrayed, rejected and abandoned. Was it easy no but I kept the right mindset and perspective, I see the positive in everything good or bad and I embraced life. I have seen God's mighty hands at work in my life, my family and my ministry. This is all about the process, God is a faithful God. Thank God there is no lack only by the grace of God. I have forgiven all who have done me wrong. We are thriving by the grace of God and soaring because we are eagles. See yourselves like God see you my friends and keep soaring.

Things may not have turn out the way we wanted or hoped but God is still a good God. The process is the most painful and challenging aspect but it is also rewarding. There is purpose in pain. The definition of process: A series of actions or steps taken in order to achieve a particular end. The process is the hardest but the best. If it was our will, we would not go through the pain but we must go through the process. Some of the food we eat has to be processed before eaten, so it is important for the process to take its course.

When we examine the potter's story: if the potter is not satisfied or if the clay is marred he will put it back in the fire or on the potter's wheel until it comes out to the desired state (Jeremiah 18 KJV). We must not give up or bend under the pressure of the process. It is a part of our destiny.

Notice that the stiffest tree is most easily cracked, while the bamboo or willow survives by bending with the wind."
- Bruce Lee

The willow survives because it does not resist the wind. So should we be through the different processes and seasons of life. The process is inevitable, with determination and a resilient mindset will lead us to victory. Your destiny is bright and the enemy is aware of this, he will try and stop the process but he cannot push in the process. Call for back-up in the process.

Notes

NOTES

3

The Lord Is On Your Side

Scripture: Exodus 14:14

The Lord will fight for you, you need only to be still.

In life we are faced with different situations and circumstances but God's promises are true. Whatever the situation or season in your life, God wants you to be still and He will fight for you.

Prayer, praise and worship is a weapon and they must be utilized in spiritual battles because they are most effective. The Lord will fight for you, just be still. God is at work in your situation, He is a mountain mover and He works best with impossibilities. He has never lost a battle. He is the Lion of the Tribe of Judah. He is your deliverer. Just be still.

I remember when I went through a season in my life, if it had not been for God I would not be here to pen these lines but thanks be to God for His grace and mercy which brought me through. Now thankfully, I am at a better place to assist someone on their journey. To God be all the Glory.

In everything we ought to trust God, He is faithful and is working behind the scene on our behalf. Circumstances may have occurred that truly are unfair and unkind but God ask us to just be still and He will fight our battles for us.

Prayer: Father in Heaven, as your Word said, "you will fight for us, we need just to be still. Help us Lord to be still as you fight for us in Jesus' Name Amen.

"Music cheers the heart, the way a bouquet of flower cheers the soul"

Chapter Four

Turning Your Worry In to Worship

Worship has been a lifestyle and how did I truly get to this point. I am telling my story not to solicit sympathy but I hope it will help someone on their journey to have the right perspective and be very optimistic about life. I was born and grown up in a Christian home, with my mom and dad under the same roof. They were married for over Thirty (30) years. As a matter of fact my parents are believers of Jesus Christ but I never had a relationship with God, when I was running to church with my parents. I was going to church to please my parents. Later in life, I was in pursuit for an encounter with God. I did have an encounter and my life took a 360 degree turn. I invest daily in my spiritual gym, feeding and nourishing my soul with the Word, so I am never spiritually anaemic. Christ is my reason for living and my only Source.

"Emotion is 'recognition'. When treasured moments are identified in the jungle of our personal history during a visual or aural encounter, we capture magic sparks from our past, arousing flashes of insight and revealing an inner flare. These instants of recognition may rekindle enthralling emotion and fulfilling inspiration."
-Erik Pevernagie

Something happened in my life that changed my life's trajectory completely and thanks be to God it did. I got married at Twenty Three (23) years of age. My husband was my cheerleader. He was just a good husband then all hell broke loose but it shaped and transformed my life positively and spiritually. I ran to God in my pain and disbelief. I went through silent pain and real emotional trauma. I pretended and sugar coated my marriage and showed the best face for Twenty Two years (22), I was abused emotionally and physically but I kept it within the four walls of my home. My marriage has transformed my life positively and now I am a beautiful worshiper, thanks be to God. Fitz thank you for being a part of my history and thank God for a great destiny.

Being a very private person and was never sharing my experience or pain with anyone I just prayed and cried to God daily. Driving to work I was crying, no tears came flowing but I sniffled and sniffled because I did not want my tears to flow so anyone would ask me what was the problem. Through all of this, God has truly been faithful to me. I have two wonderful sons, I thank God daily for them because out of every bad situation comes good. Thanks be to God.

"Don't let life affect your worship;
let your worship effect life".
-LaMar Broschman

My marriage broke, it ended up in divorce and I can still say thank God because He is truly a faithful God. He kept me through so much trauma caused by my marriage. God has given me such great peace, joy and strength in all of this. God removes all my pain; now my pain is transformed into purpose. Currently, I am serving as a Minister in the church and I can truly look back and thank God for those moments I cried myself to sleep in His arms because I knew for a fact that He was working behind the scenes for my good and yes thank God He delivered me. All I need to do is trust the Potter. I am truly an overcomer.

I took responsibility for my life and invested in my future and stayed in the church. I turned all my worry into worship. I reinvented and recreated myself because it was all temporary inconveniences. I maintained control of my mind by the grace of God and I am determined to stay focus and work towards achieving my goals. I will continue to thrive for good success.

My battles are won on my knees. Praise is a weapon and I am a warrior for God, that's how I got my victory, through my praise. I worship God wherever I go. God is my source and the moment I prayed, I told, God He intervenes into whatever I am dealing with. Some of life's experience leaves me in awe. I went to the supermarket and while waiting in the line, I was just there dancing to a beautiful song of praise. I was noticed by a lady and she shouted, "way to go!!" I believe worshipping God brings so much peace and solace not only to us but those around us.

"God has two dwellings; one in heaven and the other in a meek and thankful heart."
- Izaak Dalton

My house is known for praise, worship and prayer. I find peace in serving Jesus Christ. I love to journal, and I recommend this for everyone. In order to move ahead write down your dream and stay focus to ensure it comes to fruition. When we allow God to lead and guard our dream and vision, it will catapult you into your divine destiny and helping you achieving your goals, dreams and aspiration. Just worship. What we lost will come back to us through worship. Always be on your guard and be alert guarding the promise of God by praying without ceasing. Don't die with that unwritten book or your unfulfilled business plans within you. Take action NOW.

Rejoice evermore. Pray without ceasing. In every thing give thanks: for this is the will of God in Christ Jesus concerning you. 1 Thessalonians 5:16-18 (KJV)

Being a carrier of the Holy Anointing of God we are no more ordinary individuals. We have been tried because the mantle of the Holy anointing of God is placed on us. We receive the promise of God and have been processed by trials.

We have to empathize with others, after we have passed through a setback, we have gained more experience and we are more mature, our attitude changes positively to those who may be hurting and we are now readily available to assist others. God is seeking people like you and me in the Kingdom, someone He can trust and rely on. As we make ourselves available, may we seek more of the anointing and desire the things of God, He will not refuse an available vessel.

Turning our worry into worship, brings us to a place of intimacy with God. Intimacy with God, takes our focus off our situation and points us to have a relationship with Him.

We are talking to everyone except God. We need to talk to the Lord about everything, He is waiting to hear from us. When we talk to God about everything He helps us to make wise and right choices and decisions. Knowledge is power, let's continue to study the Word and make it applicable to our lives on a daily basis. Invite someone to fellowship with the Saviour, share your faith. The same way we communicate with our spouse and our children, the Lord wants to communicate with us. Communication takes place both ways. When we pray, we should listen for what the Lord is saying to us. Get away from the noise, intimacy with God is what is required to see changes in our lives.

"Prayer is the most essential way to cultivate intimacy with God"

We are set apart for a specific purpose. Being purpose driven, we are on this earth for a purpose. Nothing can kill purpose, keep on improving our walk and talk with God. As a worshiper, I have learnt to worship God in every situation. I have shared my experience, when I was bullied so badly in school and all the verbal tornado hurled at me. My only comfort was Jesus Christ, I shared it with no one, not even my parents. I suffered in silence. I was ridiculed and humiliated by my classmates because of my visible scars. This was very painful but God brought me through all those challenging times.

Intimacy with God is required to see us through challenging time because as long as we are alive we are going to be faced with some sort of challenges. It's our attitude that is going to determine if we will become bitter or better, the latter is the right choice. When we turn our worry into worship, everything change and even others will notice there is a change in us. There will be an aura about us. When God does a work on us, we are transformed from the inside out. We will exude the fruit of the spirit.

But the fruit of the spirit is love, joy, peace, forbearance, kindness, 23 gentleness and self-control. Against such there is no law. Galatians 5:22-23 (KJV)

It is only through a relationship with the Holy Spirit we will be able to be carriers of the anointing. The anointing destroys and breaks the yoke. The anointing is costly, it does not come cheap. Everyone who is anointed had to pay a price. It is a sacrificial relationship that gives a powerful and life changing experience of the anointing. Brokenness is required for us to be anointed or to be equipped with the authority for service. A prayerless Christian, is a powerless Christian. I am often times told that I am anointed and I humbly say, thank You Lord for choosing to anoint me. Thank God for anointing me, I am now a vessel anointed to help others.

The difference in our walk, is our talk. In our deportment, our mannerism and our personality will be changed because we are no ordinary person, we are a force to reckon with, with the anointing of God. The end result is the glory but no one knows your story. We all have made some bad decisions, may I re-iterate, that yes we all have made some bad decisions maybe great or small but because of Christ's atoning Blood has blot out our transgressions. We are redeemed and forgiven as long as we ask for, forgiveness. Thank God for His unmerited favour. His undeserved favour and love has made us whole.

What gives me the most hope every day is God's grace; knowing that his grace is going to give me the strength for whatever I face, knowing that nothing is a surprise to God.
- Rick Warren

Turning our worry into worship causes us to seek for the anointing of God. When an anointed individual speaks or ministers, you can know for sure that, that individual was with the Saviour and has a prayer life. As we go about our daily businesses, we can identify these giants of faith. It is a concerted effort and a collaborative effort of the Pastor the shepherd to feed the sheep with the Word of God and to foster and harness such love for God that it leads to a mighty revival and awakening.

Worship while you wait, is a strategy to defeat the plans and tactics of the enemy.

Be aware that once God has a plan, the enemy formulates a plan with his agents to try derail the plan of God for your life but the promise from God is sure. It may seem like it is not coming to pass but it will and it must because God cannot lie.

My friends worship, worship, worship, while you wait. God is fighting for you. We were created only for the purpose to praise God. Our bodies are the temple of the Lord. Praise and worship is a weapon and must be executed accordingly. The enemy is intimated by a worshiper. Let the praise from your mouths flow like a stream. Open your mouths and praise the Lord! Our blessing is locked up in our mouths. Praise the Lord, hallelujah. The Lord deserves all the glory and honour. He is worthy, hallelujah, He is the Alpha and Omega. The beginning and the end.

To carry the atmosphere of God's Glory is to extend it to the whole earth
Sunday Adelaja

I take this opportunity to encourage you to activate your altar, if it is inactive. Talk to God on a daily and consistent basis, meditate on His Word. Keep Christ at the center of our hearts and minds, that is the only way we can stay connected is by prayer and meditation. Father in Heaven, come and abide, come and dwell, come and tabernacle with us dear Lord. As believers, it is imperative that we are consistent as worshipers. A worshipful life is hard to be concealed because individuals are living in an overflow. An overflow life is easily identifiable. It comes out in worship and the way we relate to each other. A true believer is not arrogant, rude, boastful, proud or mean spirited/unkind. A true believer exudes and exhibits the anointing and the fruit of the spirit is demonstrated.

Embrace the challenges and struggles that you face,

all of which are vehicles to our divine destiny. Make the necessary progress, take the leap of faith. Invest in ourselves and achieve our God-given destiny. Declare the promises of God over your life daily. Help someone on their quest to victory. Each one reach one, each one teach one.

Turning our worry into worship gives us freedom. May we all turn our worry into worship.

NOTES

NOTES

4

No lack

Scripture: Phillipians 4:19

But my God shall supply all your need according to his riches in Glory by Christ Jesus.

My friend, God shall supply ALL your needs according to His riches in Glory by Christ Jesus. What a promise! This a time for a praise break: Thank you Jesus, hallelujah I am standing on your promises. God is a provider. He is Jehovah Jireh, with Him there is no lack, thank you Jesus. As you are reading this, you are not reading it by chance, it is Divine. I decree and declare a Supernatural anointing of breakthrough and overflow of everything good in Jesus' Name.

Our needs vary based on our circumstances, maybe you need to see your son/daughter surrender their lives to God or turn from a lifestyle of the sinful nature. A spouse to return home, you may be needing a car or a house, hoping to be married and starting your family. You may backslidden, trust God, whatever your needs are God will supply according to His riches in Glory by Christ Jesus. God has a perfect plan and timing for everything good for your life.

Prayer: Father in Heaven, I trust you because you are a faithful God, you never fail because that is not in your nature and for this I give you thanks in Jesus' Name Amen.

"Flowers makes everything beautiful."
-Ann Marie Bolton

CHAPTER FIVE

Endure Your Season

The different seasons of my life are very interesting, as painful as some were, God has never left my side and I never left His will. I lived out my passion, I truly enjoy motivating others because in doing so I motivate myself. Some seasons are more difficult than some, just as it is in the natural, so it is in the spiritual. I have prayed and cried expecting God to change my situation. My situation was changed yes but not the way I expected it. When I am faced with a challenge, I ensure that I win first in my mind then it manifest itself. It is important to keep the engine of our minds engaged.

In the depth of winter, I finally learned that within me there lay an invincible summer
- Albert Camus

In life what we are expecting and needing in our lives, God choose not to grant our wish or prayers because He knows it can be devastating but when He gives us according to His will, we get the best. This we cannot see immediately but as the years go by we realize that God was keeping us from ourselves. As in (Ecclesiastes 3:1-8 KJV)

Some very important points to remember in achieving a divine promise we must endure our season. Thrive in your season and remain faithful. It may be a vision that is bigger than you and you are in that season thinking how is this going to happen. I do not have the money and you are talking to yourself negatively. Don't let the lack of evidence, talk you out of God's promise. Endure your season with praise. Be enthusiastic and model your dream and vision and be bold in all the seasons of your life. You are equipped with seeds of greatness.

By God's design we will lose somethings and we will receive something better. The design of the promise is for you to receive the best and this is God's best not our best. God has a plan for our lives. It is a beautiful plan and he is beckoning to us to come unto Him, with all our cares and concerns. He will remove all your imperfections and make you into vessels of honour as He has promised.

"You can't reach your potential by remaining in a past due season. Your breakthrough is coming. Strongholds are breaking. Get Ready!
- Germany Kent

You may be concerned about things you have done in the past, the truth is we all have done somethings in the past that we would not want to repeat or share with anyone. This is life. Our past is building blocks for the future. There will always be challenges on the journey, from we are alive we are going to be faced with challenges. No one can sugar coat life's journey, life happen. We have to be strong and surround ourselves with people who are strong. Resilience is the key in life, you will survive. Turn your wounds into wisdom.

"The oak fought the wind and was broken, the willow bent when it must and survived."
- Robert Jordan

Your past is necessary for the future. The past is what

gives us experience and maturity. Without those experiences we would not be able to help someone else, in the same or similar circumstances. We can therefore relate and encourage others effectively because we had gone through it ourselves. Challenges and storms in our lives are vehicles to our divine destiny and should be embraced. Promise and problems walk hand in hand. Are we going to run or shy away, or quit no we are not.

Being ignorant of the fact that we sometimes block our blessing by complaining or grumbling and because of our murmuring it takes a longer time to be fulfilled. A heart of gratitude is one we all should model. We need to get out of our own way, we are blocking our destiny and so are the company that we keep. Keeping it positive is most important for growth. We must get out of the way so God can have His way. The enemy is going to throw everything at us to frustrate us on the journey but we must persevere in order to fulfil and achieve our goals.

"What we think is a breakdown, is only a breakthrough. Whatever you may be going through, see it as an opportunity to propel yourself to the limitless heights in existence."
- Angie Karan

I have praised my way through and past my circumstances. At times when I should be sad, I just started to praise God. I just burst out in worship, this is very therapeutic. I encourage you to try this soothing method of erasing our pains. A song of praise heals wounds and mend broken hearts and dreams. Are you broken or disheartened? I implore you to just break forth in praise and adoration unto God.

We sometimes say we are waiting on God but God is waiting on us. Sometimes our selfish agenda gets in the way of the agenda of the Creator. We can be our worst enemy. We must be aware of the season and time we are in. Whatever tactics or schemes of the enemy that the enemy is trying to use to stop, thwart and block us on our journey will be rendered powerless in Jesus' Name Amen. The enemy is defeated by the Blood of Jesus Christ.

The spell and curse is broken. Every cyclical pattern orchestrated by the enemy is broken and destroyed by the Precious Blood of Jesus Christ. On the journey we will tested by our Father, for the sake of purification. This can be very rigid but we must stay the course because it is for our own good. We should never go around complaining about our process. On the journey we should erase procrastination from our lives completely. Do not put off today for tomorrow.

"A year from now you may wish you had started today."
- Karen Lamb

We must endure our season, distraction can cause derailment. One must be focus and beware of posers. These are people who pretends to be friends but are true distraction on our journey. Be vigilant and alert on your journey. Be enthusiastic

about your journey, it's contagious. With much diligence and patience, working consistently. Sowing good seeds and most importantly, sowing on good soil. God's got you.

Be vibrant on the journey, when asked how we are doing, our response should be excellent, blessed and highly favoured or outstanding. Set yourself apart by being enthusiastic and motivated. Our goal should be to cheer and impact everyone we come in contact with. Be admired for your positivity. People do not want to be around wimps and whiners.

You are number one and tell yourself that on a daily basis. Remind yourself daily of that by looking in the mirror and reaffirm yourself and believe it. Daily positive affirmation on the journey is of utmost importance. You are loved, you are above and never beneath, I am a conqueror, I am a millionaire, wealth and riches are in my house, etc. Invest in yourself, physical exercise is a must, when we endure our season we do everything to get us through each day and this should be viewed positively.

"Our goals can only be reached through a vehicle of plan, in which we must fervently believe, and upon which we must vigorously act. There is no other route to success."
- Stephen A. Brenan

We must pay attention to the prompting of the Holy Spirit, or one may call it our gut feeling on our journey. We do not want to miss an opportunity because we are not paying attention. It is imperative that we pay attention in the class of life because we do not want to repeat a lesson. This can be real detrimental to our progress and future self. Please note, God's plan for our life is to have good success. We were created by God, He loves us and He wants the best for us. We must take advantage of each opportunity to grow and get the most out of ourselves. If we do we will remain at the top in our career and choices we make.

We must declare the promise of God out of our own mouths. Blessings are in our mouths. God is waiting on us to open our mouths and declare His promises over our lives. In the natural it may look like we fail but in the spiritual we are successful. God has given His angels charge over us to protect us on the journey. For He shall give His angels charge over thee to keep thee in all thy ways. (Psalm 91:11 KJV). What great promise and benefit from God our Heavenly Father.

On the journey we must exude confidence. Hold your heads up high and think big and dream big. Be optimistic and build each other up to do the good things of life. Be a people person. I have practiced all my life to be a people person and because of that people enjoys my company. Be your best on the journey, if you are going through something in your personal life, everyone doesn't have to know, it's between you and who you decide to share it with. Maintain your standard and keep raising the bar higher. Be a role model, people are depending you. When someone choose to be unkind do no repay evil for evil, that person is hurting that's why they were unkind to you, do not take it personal.

Harsh words can cause more wounds than sticks and stones Dada J.P. Vaswani

Growing up I wanted to be a teacher sadly, I took a detour into the secretarial/management field and I still think I am to pursue my dream. Never allow your attitude to compromise your altitude. Love yourself so much that anyone doesn't love you back it doesn't affect you negatively. God will do everything to refine us and build His character in us. Having the right attitude in trials and challenges is a sure way of God refining us. When we work with God, we will come forth as pure gold. You are a gem.

"A gem cannot be polished without friction, nor a man be perfected without trials" - Lucius Annaeus Seneca

A gemstone has to be cut and polished in order for it to become or be used as a jewelry. So is the individual or a believer will be polished by trials but rest assured with the right attitude, you will become a masterpiece. We all have things in our lives that need to be fine-tuned. Some of us are not fully surrendered and as a consequence, some rough edges in our attitude are surfaced every now and then. It is good when these hidden flaws are revealed because they can be dealt with and corrected in the light. In the darkness it is developed as in the negative of a photograph.

"Character is like a photograph, it develops in darkness"
Yousuf Karsh

When we have a vision or a dream, God opens favour in our lives. When we are walking and living in favour the impossible happens. Favour chases us down daily, I went to the store, waiting in a long line and the cashier said "may I help the other customer," I was the next customer and was thankful for such kind gesture. If we just slow down and pause and look through the corridors of our lives we too can testify of God's daily provision of favour.

Another example of God's daily favour and provision: In 2011 my son was preparing to sit his CXC and had his Student Base Assignment (SBA) saved on a thumb drive. We were travelling from Westmoreland to Montego Bay. The main road to Montego Bay was flooded with water, so we had to detour through Bethel Town to get into Montego Bay. Enroute to Montego Bay we heard a sound under the car. We stopped (my son and I) came out of the car in Bethel Town in the morning about 7:00 a.m. He had the thumb drive on his lap and when he came out it fell, not noticing we drove off.

It was now time for me to drop him off at college, when I did, he asked me for the thumb drive, then we found out that the unthinkable thing has happened. The thumb drive fell in Bethel Town when we stopped to check on sound on the car. This you can imagine was devastating. I did what I know to do, I prayed and went to work. The SBA is a very important part for CXC in the Caribbean. We trusted God that He is going to work something out.

"Whoever fear God, shall find favour"
- Lailah Giffy Akita

I did my days work, went to pick up my son and we started on our journey that was like 7:00 p.m. This road I must tell you is a very busy thoroughfare. When we got to the location where we stopped in the morning we stopped back there in the evening. Another car came and stopped adjacent to ours and asked us what was wrong and we explained. I am excited….. this is God at work…do you believe in miracle?

We all know how small a thumb drive is, to my surprise the lady said she found it, this is a miracle, she went inside her house and brought the thumb drive to us. Nothing ran over it, it was just as he lost it, he found it back. Friends, God is a miracle working God. The road is a very busy thoroughfare and it was not damaged, God is a good God. He is a faithful God. My son later submitted the SBA from the same thumb drive, sat the CXC Examination and got a One in the same subject Information Technology (I.T.), God is an AWESOME God. I am still rejoicing and is forever grateful for God's faithfulness and favour. When God favours you everyone is at peace with you.

Our presence change the atmosphere. Our presence change the situation. The favour of God is powerful because of the dream God places in our hearts.

Notes

Notes

5

Fear Not

Scripture Isaiah 41:10

So do not fear, for I am with you; do not be dismayed, I am your God. I will strengthen you and help you; I will uphold you with my righteous right hand.

God has commanded us in the scripture that we should not fear. God will intervene on our behalf and make us victorious and not victims. Why should we not fear? God is with us. What comfort and confidence we find in the Word, who is Jesus Christ. God wants us to remind Him of His promises to us.

Yes, we must remind God of His promises to us when faced with challenges and when we are going through the different seasons of our lives. I can personally say, had it not been for God on my side, I just do not know where I would be but thank you Lord for your grace and mercy.

We are not inevitable of difficulties, they will come but rest assured God is with you. God is our strength in weakness. He will, yes He will strengthen you and help you. Look to God and have no fear, seek His face daily and ask Him to guide and protect you, so there will be no fear because the Holy Spirit dwells within. Our body is the temple of the Holy Ghost and no fear but faith lives on the inside.

When we look around on the changing time one may want to think and be fearful but with God on our side, we are sheltered and safe in his arms. Fear not my brothers and sisters God is with you.

Prayer: Father in Heaven I will not fear because you are my Helper and you uphold me with your righteous right hand. Thank you Lord in Jesus' Name Amen.

"Flowers are like sunshine on a bleak day"
-Ann Marie Bolton

Chapter Six

It Is Not Over

After Twenty Two (22) years of marriage and it ended in divorce, I was so devastated. I held on to the marriage vows because it was a covenant made before man and God and I held it sacred as it should be. My husband and I met when I was attending school in Montego Bay and by coincidence we ended up in the same work environment and then the fire in my heart started and the rest is history. At the age of Twenty Three (23) I got married to the man I thought would be my life partner but my husband took a detour.

"Divorce isn't such a tragedy. A tragedy's staying in an unhappy marriage, teaching your children the wrong things about love. Nobody ever died of divorce."
– Jennifer Weiner

For the most part of our marriage, my husband was overseas making ends meet for us his family, which we are eternally grateful for, I must add he really loved his family. Then something inevitable happened. The day my marriage went up in smoke, my husband called me and said at 5:00p.m. that same evening, I should give him a call.

"It is your passion that empowers you to be able to do the thing you were created to do."
- T.D. Jakes

As a wife, I was submissive to my husband, so I returned the call and only to my surprise he told me, I quote "my love for you have died and I have divorced you," I said what! That was tough but thanks be to God I did nothing stupid because God is always with me, so He has prepared me for this moment.

The sad part is my husband told me about the divorce at my own expense. He told me to call him and I did. As time goes by and healing takes its course, I was able to laugh at it. I told my children and they were traumatized for years and to be honest, to this date they are devastated. My children grew up and I instilled the disciplines, values and attitude in them and thank God, they grew up to be dignified young men, without a dad under the same roof.

"A courageous soul is the one who dares to learn, grow and evolve through the highway of an emotional disaster"
- Dhiraj Kumar Raj

The lesson I have learnt out of my failed marriage is "It's not over". Live your life with great expectations, expecting the best and you will attract it. There is greatness on you. Be hungry and thrive for success. Never Give Up! There will always be failures in our lives but our failures are building blocks to our success. Please pay

attention in life because there were signs, which I was not paying attention to because as a husband and father, he loved us his family but life gives us things we must deal with, as unfortunate as it is I am not bitter just better.

Quitting is never an option. Never give up! It doesn't matter how bad your situation or circumstances are, find someone you can confide in and vent. Talk about your life experience it will help you as you encourage someone else. Be positive in everything you do. Be impactful. It's not over. Come on this journey with me and take charge of your destiny. Life is cyclical. Every negative situation shall pass. We have sunshine and we have rain. Amazing God we serve. Use your life to be a light.

The most important person in my life is my Heavenly Father

Notes

Notes

6

Rejoice

Scripture: Psalm 37:4

Delight thyself in the LORD; and he shall give thee the desires of thine heart.

Whatever you do be delightful, be happy, be filled with joy and peace. Delight thyself in the LORD and He shall give thee the desires of thine heart. What are you desiring of the LORD? What is your attitude in whatever you are desirous for?

This is very important, we must be joyous in serving God because the joy of the Lord is our strength. Happiness is contagious, spread the joy in whatever you do and others will crave and want what you have. If you need joy, give joy away. You need a breakthrough help someone get their breakthrough. It is all about sowing and reaping.

The LORD shall give you the desires of your heart, you only need to be delightful and trust him. I will live victoriously, I am anointed to prosper and to enjoy the benefits of what God has provided for me. When Jesus went to the cross, he did it all you for you and I. Make it up your minds to be happy and delight thyself in the Lord.

He made us to occupy this earth and to delight in the things that he created for us here on earth. Everything is at our disposal, it is for us to use them wisely and enjoy safe passage while we delight ourselves in the LORD. As we serve and make disciples let us be delighted as we share Christ with others.

Prayer: Father in Heaven, help us to take you at your Word and be delightful in you oh as you give us the desires of our heart in Jesus' Name Amen.

"Look for the flowers in a forest of weeds and cling to the beautiful flowers."
-Ann Marie Bolton

Chapter Seven

Building Bridges and not Barriers

Our relationship with God is first and foremost. As the scripture states, seek ye first the Kingdom of God and everything else will be added unto you (Matthew 6:33). God will connect us with the right individuals who aligns with our God-given destiny, if we first seek Him. When we take charge of our destiny, we will surround ourselves with the right people who will motivate and encourage us on our journey. Destiny helpers will locate us and propel us into our destiny. I have worked at three work places for my life. I am stable and well rounded. I look for the best in people and because of that I gained and attract friends quite easily. My personality is warm, fuzzy and friendly because of this, I was always admired and held in high regard.

Greatness is not measured by the walls
we build but by the bridges.
- DaShanne Stokes

I worked at this particular establishment for many years. I worked for many years as an Executive Secretary and continues to upgrade myself aiming at self-actualization. In this organization I was faced with much challenges but this was a time of professional and personal growth for me, so I stayed focused. As uncomfortable as it was I viewed all those challenges as opportunity and I soared. I was awarded with the Image Award for the company. My voice was the signature of the company. To date I call them my family. I am a consistent high performer and I am known for my professionalism in the work place. I believe in excellence and I executed my duties accordingly.

Due to my professionalism the company retained their customers for years. I built bridges and not walls everywhere I go. Relationship is very important to me because we need people to survive. I was talked about in a positive way by everyone except for the people with competitive spirit. I believe in exceeding the customers expectation and knowing that the customer is always right and treated everyone with equal respect and dignity, brought me to a place of much positive recognition.

"It doesn't matter who you are, where you come from. The ability to triumph begins with you. Always."
- Oprah Winfrey

There is a proverb "show me your company and I will tell you who you are." Moral of this quote is our association or friends dictates our future and become an active force in our lives. We must aim to achieve more and to do so we must build relationships with like-minded and vision-minded individuals. Share your vision and get help to fulfil your vision. Relationships are very important. We must build a network with people who will stretch us and take us out of our comfort zone. No one gets where they want to be while sitting in their comfort zone. Take charge of your destiny. Find people who will support you. Build relationships. Live your life you deserve it. You owe it to yourself.

"A ship in Harbour is safe but that is not what ships are built for"
- Alan Henry

Do not procrastinate, act on your dream, build relationship and do not waste valuable time. Life is very fragile, be happy and work on your goals. Build relationship with people who can develop you spiritually, personally and professionally. It is very important that you surround yourself with people who celebrate you. Look for WINNERS and not whiners. Celebrate yourself. Design your life strategically to WIN.

You need to choose your association according to your vision
- Onyi Anyado

There are some people we must not connect with they are emotional vampires. They are too negative, they can walk into a dark room and start to develop. Stay away from negative environments, they are not healthy for your growth. Seek for employment not just a J.O.B. (Journey of the Broke). Attract only (OQP) only quality people. Get ready for an overflow of God's blessings. Build nourishing relationships that bring the best out of you. Don't waste your mental muscle on thinks that does not develop the qualities in you to become a winner. Bridges connect while barriers separate us. United we stand and divided we fall. Togetherness is key. One can be suffering in silence, I did that for years because I did not trust anyone to share my story with. I was bullied, humiliated and ridiculed but God saw me through.

"Go where you are celebrated, not tolerated. If they can't see the real value of you, it's time for a new star."
- Unknown

The anointing and intimacy with God gives us a heart of compassion and empathy. It gives sweet and everlasting peace, which is obvious even to the impaired. The anointing of God allows us to cultivate peace with and helps us in building relationships. You are selfless and peaceful with the anointing of God. When people are frantic and scared an anointed person is at complete peace. Nothing or no one can disturb this peace, this peace is not man made. The peace that God gives diffuses all conflicts and strife. It dwells in a vessel that is chosen and equipped by the Holy Spirit, the Comforter to carry out His work here on earth.

And the peace of God, which passeth all understanding, shall keep your hearts and minds through Christ Jesus.
Philippians 4:7 (KJV)

I choose to live the way I do building bridges and not barriers. We need a friend and a confidante. There will comes a time when we need someone to assist us or just to talk to. This is very important for our mental health. When people sit and over think this is where the problems lie. Stay connected with people, relatives or friends. Being a part of a community namely: church or a social club is healthy, in this way one can make lasting friends.

We must always think of ways to surround ourselves with people of value and surround ourselves with positive people. Stay away from thought poisoning communication (gossip). Gossip makes one small. Be an encourager and bless people with your words. Build relationship that will catapult and propel us into our destiny.

Treat your relationship as if you are growing the most beautiful sacred flower. Keep watering it, tend to the roots, and always make sure the petals are full of colour and are never curling. Once you neglect your plant, it will die, as will your relationship.
- Suzy Kassem

I have seen where I made friends until I was comfortable enough to share my scars with, even now to record in a memoir. I have truly come along way, all of this has to do with maturity. Immaturity can cause us to make bad decisions. We may have to face things on our own and suffer in silence when we do not build relationship and trust anyone to share with. I understand because I can relate, I suffered in silence because when I was bullied I never shared it with my parents or anyone.

If at the time I had built a relationship I would then be comfortable to share it. My advice to you, do not suffer in silence this can be very devastating. I remember when I told a co-worker that I lost some of my hair, she turned and asked me, "so where did you get that confidence from," because I am a very confident person sometimes it is misinterpreted as being proud and arrogant. I know what God has done for me and I am indeed grateful, so I wear my blessings well. Thank You Jesus!

Notes

Notes

7

Prosperity

Scripture Jeremiah 29:11

For I know the plans I have for, "declares the LORD," plans to prosper you and not to harm you, plans to give you hope and a future.

Your destiny is secure because God has great plans for us. I decree and declare that God has great plans for our lives according to His Word. Since you are reading this book you are blessed and highly favoured. God has great plans and purposes for our lives all we need to do is abide in His will. Nothing good will God withhold from us. We are His children and He is our Heavenly Father and that makes us special.

We have a bright future, each waking moment God has a mighty miracle with our names engraved on it. He will not let us down. God is faithful and true all we need to do is believe. God will give us the strength we need for the bright future He has prepared for us. Go ahead and live your life boldly. You are unstoppable. Your dreams and aspirations will come to fruition.

My friend, God has a great plan for your life. Do you believe? He will never fail, this is what he has promised and he will deliver. Trusting Jesus really pays, believe his Word. As we paint our minds with the Word of God and engrave faith on our minds as beautiful roses. Let us etch it in our minds that God has a great plan for our lives.

Prayer: Father in Heaven, thank you that you have great plans for our lives in Jesus' Name Amen.

"As beautiful as roses are, they grow through the dirt."
-Ann Marie Bolton

CHAPTER EIGHT

Don't Let Your Dream Die

Setbacks make us stronger, challenges makes us stronger. It's our attitude towards our problems and challenges that's going to make us or break us. Choose the positive. Never give up on your dream. You may feel depleted and your energy is drained but fail forward and persevere that's what gives us strength. Life is a process and there is a lesson that we must learn from life's experiences. Before things get better, they will get worst. Don't let your dream die. You got to be a risk taker. Make your dream become a reality. Fight the good fight of faith and maintain a positive attitude always. There are benefits in being positive.

You are either supporting the vision or supporting division
-Saji Ljiyemi

Be careful of dream killers. They will discourage you instead of encouraging you. Negative energy you do not need in your life. Climbing my career ladder, I had to stay away from negative people. I connect only with positive people. Visualize yourself and invest greatly in yourself and success is sure. You are here on purpose for a purpose. We must have the mindset of a billionaire. We must soar as eagles and employ that winning attitude to keep our dreams alive. God will move the enemy and the opposition out of your way for you to fulfil God's plan for your life. God knows how to do a quick work. Now is the key to success.

"Never give up hope. All things are working for your good. One day, you'll look back on everything you've been through and thank God for it." - Germany Kent

Your angels are busy working it out for you. Whatever you are believing God for, receive it by FAITH. Is this dream or promise bigger than you? Is your past getting in your way negatively? Let your past be your platform to soar and be successful. Never settle for mediocrity, we are blessed and highly favoured. On our road to success, there will be a lot of distractions. Distractions or obstacles are designed to derail us. Let's pray bold prayers and not weak prayers or praying amiss.

Live your vision and demand your success - Steve Maraboli

We thank God for His unmerited favour. We must be intentional and work towards achieving our goals and our dreams. Remove every fear, remember fear tolerated is faith contaminated. We must have faith in God because He is a faithful God. Our dream is for a set time, in God's perfect timing it will come to pass, do your part in writing the vision (Habakkuk 2:2). Do your part and God will do His part. A delay with your dream is not denial.

God is equipping us in the waiting period and preparing us spiritually while we wait on the overflow of blessings. Lord thank You for blessing me indeed. You cannot pray and reach your potential by praying small prayers. God wants us to take the limits off Him. We cannot reach our potential by praying small prayers. God is waiting on us to tap into our God-given potential. God will help us in everything we do as long as it is in His will for our lives.

"Winners make habit of manufacturing their own positive expectations in advance of the event."
- Brian Tracy

There is provision in the promise of your dream. We are positioned to prosper. God gives us strength and comfort us while we wait. It is important to note that we pay attention. The Word gives direction in our waiting period. It gives clarity and it gives peace, just to name a few attributes and benefits while we wait upon God to fulfil a promise or a dream.

Your dream may not be clear to you, it may come in a parable that you do not understand. God asks us to trust Him, He will direct us to the right person for interpretation for our dream. As with Pharaoh he had two dreams (Genesis 41 KJV) only Joseph could interpret the dreams and he was the only one who gave him the correct interpretation.

The same God will direct you to someone who will give you clarity on the promise or the dream. When we have dreams to fulfil, we may have to say goodbye to the familiar in order to keep moving forward. Saying goodbye to a friend, a job, just to name a few. We have to let go to grow. He never closes a door without opening a new door.

We have to let go of the old. Everything in our lives are seasonal. God is taking us from glory to glory.

"In order to find your true potential, what you need to do is simply determine your core values, visualize the person you want to be, challenge common thought traps, and have a clear sense of your goals."
- Dr. Prem Jagyasi

When a dream is placed in our hearts, we have to visualize and actualize the promise by modeling it in every way possible. Step out in faith to accomplish your dream. Faith is an action word. God wants to move supernaturally on your behalf. Will you give Him a chance in your life? For our dream to come to fruition God will re-arrange somethings in our lives. Somethings that are viewed as priority by us are not viewed by God as priority. We are looking through our short term lens, while God is viewing our circumstances on a long-term basis. That's why we have to let God and let go. We are crowned with favour.

We are royalty, we are Kingdom citizens and we receive Kingdom favour and blessings. For us to accomplish our dreams we have to let go of the past. Do not allow a negative past define your future. Your destiny is Divine, God has forgiven you as long as you have asked Him to. Do not be so hard on yourself. Forgive yourself and be set free for from mental slavery. God's purposes for our lives will come to fruition. We are surrounded with God's favour like a shield. We are blessed and cannot be cursed.

Intentional living is the art of making our own choices before others choices make us - Richie Norton

Be intentional about your dream, connect or network with the right people. Try and connect with people in the same area that you would like to major or excel in. If you want to be a Teacher, partner with Teachers and the same is true for all your career or something you are passionate about. We have to stop self-sabotage and erase procrastination out of our lives and move forward towards your vision.

Choose your friends carefully, waste no time with people who are not making any progress in life. That is not healthy for you. Help all those people you can, in so doing you are helping yourself.

God wants to do something great to you and through you. Avail yourself and be welling to serve. Serving others is most important for our success. Serving characterized the life of Jesus Christ. Jesus said, For even the Son of Man did not come to be served but to serve, and to give his life a ransom for many" (Mark 10:45 KJV). Jesus Christ is our great example, He was selfless (unselfish). We should not all be concerned about our own interest but the interest of others. We must be submissive to God's authority for the promise to come to fruition. Submission to God is worshiping God in spirit and in truth. In the realm of the spirit the flesh cannot stand. The flesh cannot withstand the anointing of the Holy Spirit.

Notes

Notes

8

No Weapon!

Scripture: 54:17

No weapon that is formed against thee shall proper; and every tongue that shall rise against thee in judgement thou shall condemn. This is the heritage of the servant of the Lord, and their righteousness is of me, saith the Lord.

I decree and declare no weapon – no weapon formed against thee shall prosper. God is our defence. He is our strong tower. He is our deliverer. He is our hiding place. He is our refuge. He is our Way maker. No weapons, God has our backs. No harm shall befall us. No weapon, saints of God. Hallelujah! Thank you Jesus for fighting for us.

Every evil plans, scheme, demonic assignment, tactics and devices are cancelled by the BLOOD OF JESUS CHRIST. Every stronghold is broken in Jesus' Names. Rest assured beloved saints of God, God is on our side, this is our Godly heritage. This is our Godly inheritance, Oh Glory to God. Thank you for loving us our Heavenly Father.

Prayer: Father in Heaven, thank you that you have a great plan for our lives in Jesus' Name Amen.

"Flowers prove to us we can make a positive comeback after adversity. Just keep on watering it back to life."
-Ann Marie Bolton

Chapter Nine

God Is In Control

I accepted Jesus Christ as my personal Lord and Saviour at the age of Fifteen (15). One would say that's a tender age but I am happy I did. God is my only Source and I choose to live daily to please Him. God is in control and He will allow the worst things to happen in our lives just to get our attention. Not to kill us and sometimes it can be that drastic because we were warned but we disobeyed. As children going to church it was so much fun and joy to go to church.

When we are children we seldom think of the future. This innocence leaves us free to enjoy ourselves as few adults can. The day we fret about the future is the day we leave our childhood behind.
-Patrick Rothfuss

Youth Service (NYI) was held on Friday nights and this was one of the many services we anticipated attending. It was great fun walking and talking on the roads with no fear. We had a lots of fun. When church was over, we walked as young people on the streets with no fear. No one would trouble us the only thing they spoke about in those days was duppy (ghost). When I became an adult I understood what they meant (F.E.A.R.) False Evidence Appearing Real. Growing up was fun! We had a blast as children and young people. This is the same enthusiasm I employ to my life as an adult. Faith over fear and positive thinking.

"You may not always have a comfortable life and you will not always be able to solve all of the world's problems at once but don't ever underestimate the importance you can have because history has shown us that courage can be contagious and hope can take on a life of its own."
- Michelle Obama

As we acknowledge our Creator He will guide our steps. As the Word says, his Word is a lamp unto my feet and a light unto my path (Psalm 119:105 KJV). Think Big and Do Big. Seek out positive information and connections. It's important for you to stay connected with believers. Tell your story! Never surrender to a setback, setbacks are just a set-up for a comeback to propel us forward. Take action and dig in.

Your breakthrough is coming in an unprecedented way. You are going to be the catalyst in your family. God is going to give us a net breaking blessing. God is in control and God is not limited by our capacity. He is going to allow our cups to run over with His blessings. There is a running over blessing coming your way, stay focus.

Some say if you want success surround yourself with successful people. I say if you want true and lasting success surround yourself with people of integrity.
- Charles F. Glassman

God is going to exceed our faith all we need is to keep our hearts pure and have a good attitude, treat people well and God will give us a net-breaking blessing. With God in control no evil can befall us I Decree and Declare (Isaiah 54:17 KJV) over our lives, NO WEAPON formed against shall prosper. I am living in the overflow because God is in control. God is in control and because of that I am BLESSED indeed.

Pray Big and Bold prayers and make your requests known unto God. God did not bring us into this world to be average. Joseph had God's favour and same does you and I. When we examine the life and story of Joseph, we use this term "**from the guttersmost to the uttermost**." Joseph had God's favour and because of that he was promoted from the pit to the palace. Can anyone relate to Joseph's story?

Some years ago I had a dream about myself and two persons soaring in the sky. In the dream I was leading or at the front of the other two ladies and I shouted back at them while soaring, "look to the sun/Son, look to the sun/ Son," twice and I shared the dream with the other two ladies and it was not well received. They were upset about the dream and even told others about it. But God's favour is not partial. If God declares you as a leader so shall it be. Joseph had a dream and he was hated by his brothers.

Submit to God and be at peace with him;
in this way prosperity will come to you.
- Anonymous

God's favour brings prosperity into our lives. Are you living a prosperous life? Prosperity is also for the believer. I have heard it mentioned several times about prosperity sermon but kingdom citizens must prosper because this is one of the many benefits to the believers. God is a God of providence. He is Jehovah Jireh and He wants us to live in abundance and prosperity. Lack and poverty is of the enemy and they are cancelled and destroyed by the Blood of Jesus Christ.

As I have said, I was abandoned, rejected and betrayed. I got married at a very young age. My husband of Twenty-Two (22) years threw in the towel. Thank God He never fails and in every area of my life He keeps coming through for me. Marriages should be enjoyed and not endured, some couple are suffering in silence. They could have given up but no, they never did they trusted God for sure He came through. Keep trusting and keep believing, God will change your situation positively.

That which does not kill us makes us stronger.
- Friedrich Nietzsche

The process is not comfortable, we will have to leave our comfort zone and reach for the sky. Challenge yourselves to become greater. It may look bad but the end result will be positive. We will be faced with broken promises from the human side but God will never break any of His promises to us.

These life experiences and lessons have birthed and catapulted me to another realm and another dimension in the spirit. In every trial there is a lesson to learn. We are taught these lessons to equip us to help others who need help. Thank God for choosing me to bear his Holy and precious anointing. The process turns us into spiritual giants. Every trial that comes in our lives have a beautiful lesson. We must be conscious and ask God what does he wants us to learn from the situations we encounter. When we listen to someone ministers, whether it be in Word or in song you will know that the individual is spiritually broken.

A spiritually broken person is the most compassionate and empathetic person because they have been processed rigorously. Now it is our turn to help others. Extend yourself to those who are wounded. You are now equipped to share your experiences with others. Help to sooth someone else's pain or discomfort.

"My mentor said, "Let's go do it,' not you go do it. How powerful when someone says, "Let's!"
- Jim Rohn

Be a mentor, just in case someone is hurting, they will be comfortable to confide and share it with you. Share your story and show them and tell them how God has brought you out. Be transparent and practical. When you do, you will be trusted and earn respect when you are transparent. Tell others that they can and will make it. Be kind and gentle because everyone has a battle of some sort dealing with.

You may be in traffic, someone did not let you in, in the traffic but at least another person let you in. Be kind and do not be upset or frustrated; anxiety causes wrong decisions which we will live to regret. Be patient, kind and honest, someone need to hear from you a word of encouragement. People are depending on you, they may not say it out loud but maybe one of your secret admirers because of something they see in you. Always be on your guard and be prayerful. Touch as many lives as possible. Please use this book as a manual of success. Share it with a friend, let's all succeed together.

Prove to the world that you are alive, let your words breathe life into the nostrils of the universe.
- Michael Bassey Johnson

As believers we are the light that dispels all darkness in this dismal world. Let us shine our light so others can see Christ in us and come to worship Him. We are the salt of the earth. Matt 5:13-16 (KJV). Intimacy with God and the anointing of God makes us a better person to our families and friends. We all need to seek for wisdom, knowledge and understanding. We will be easier to get along with because we are now operating as the Lord would want us to. The process is challenging but the end result is rewarding. As I have said previously, seek God, call upon Him while He is near. God is a friend who sticketh closer than a brother.

One who has unreliable friends soon comes to ruin, but there is friend who sticketh closer than a brother.
Proverbs 18:24 KJV

God is in control. He is the wheel in the middle of the wheel. Seek to be in the know. Knowledge is power when used constructively. Do your best. Be positive and wise. Be a friend. Be Kind. Be an encourager. God is in control and He cares for you. When we are favoured by God we walk around with a chip of greatness in us.

SOAR!

Notes

Notes

9

We Are The Called

Scripture: Romans 8:28

And we know that all things work together for good to them that love God, to them who are the called according to his purpose.

Hallelujah! This verse of scripture excites my spirit. And we know that all things work together for good to them that love God, to them who are the called according to his purpose.

Thank God we are the called according to His purpose. We are the called, oh praise God. We must live an intentional life daily because we are the called. God's purpose must be fulfilled, it doesn't matter what it looks like presently. Whether good or bad it is a part of the processing and in God's perfect timing it will all come together. Let us cultivate that attitude of gratitude even for the bad happenings in our lives and water the garden of our souls with God's Word.

Prayer: Our Father in Heaven, thank you that we are the called, please help us to live accordingly until eternity in Jesus' Name Amen.

"Flowers go through storm and hurricanes yet they survive. Human beings encounter adversity and adversary and they complain." Be like the flower and survive your storm.
-Ann Marie Bolton

Chapter Ten

Encounter to Empower

Have you ever come into contact with someone and it feels like you just came out of a training seminar. When we speak of encounter to empower these are the kind of encounters one would want to glean on. Positive encounters are life changing. Each encounter should be impactful and rewarding. As people and children of light when we enter a dark room or living in this dark world our presence should make a difference by bringing a ray of hope to people who are drowning in their guilt. That's why each encounter should be impactful.

Be ready to give an encouraging word, practice to live in the overflow. People are hurting and need to hear a kind word. Be mindful of each contact. When I was traumatized I just wanted to hear the positive and never to hang around negative people. I have made it up in my mind that it doesn't matter what, I have be positive. I often time said, even the ground I walk on is Positive. Treating people with respect encourage people to want to be around you. Invest in yourself and others. Our approach to life has significant impact on ourselves and others.

You only have one first chance to make one first impression that lasts a life time
- J. K. Rowling

As the saying goes the first impression last. Should we be a complainer no one would want to be in our company for a second and more so most times no one will entertain a complainer. People choose to be in the company of a positive motivated and enthusiastic person. We ought to be enthusiastic about our lives. Life is beautiful and must be seen and lived accordingly. Going on a trip, a cruise or something to entertain and cheer the heart.

I am an introvert and with that being said, I am not concerned about what people think of me. I rely solely on God and myself. My motivation is intrinsic so I do not have to be around people to be happy. I can do good, all by myself. As a people builder, I choose to uplift and build people every chance I get. One of my passions is to minister in song. I do so from a place of spiritual brokenness, in this way there is a fragrance and there is an aroma. Seeking God for more of the anointing is what matters most.

Are you impactful? It is not too late to change your mental attitude. Whatever our thought pattern is it will be reflected in our behaviour. Employ the right mental attitude and attract people to interact with you and have meaningful relations. We are to ensure we have a positive impact on each encounter.

The strength of your mind determines the quality of your life - Edmund Mbiaka

I can remember in my teenage years going to school, devotion was taking place and I happened to walk by one of the teachers, a bell was sitting on the rail of the corridor and when I passed, the bell fell. Not sure how it fell because I did not touch it and what the teacher said to me I can still remember but with no ill-feeling. "he said I am malicious," but for a teacher to say that to a student is very disturbing.

As a teacher, he should know better and to choose to use his words wisely.

For those reading this book and you have had a bad encounter please let it go, let us not hold ourselves to our past. I can agree we will remember them but only to use them as motivation and an empowerment tool. For all the scars and pains I have confronted, they now serve as building blocks to a firm foundation for a great destiny.

A successful man is one who can lay a firm foundation with the bricks others have thrown at him
- David Brinkley

Release all the negative energy it only drains the positive energy. No one wants to carry around baggage or refuse. You are not a dumpster, do not harbour any malice or bitterness. It starts right in the mind. See yourself as a star because you are a star. You are on the center stage of your life. Any thoughts that disempower you should not be tolerated. Daily empowerment is advised and should be practiced. Impactful encounter.

KEEP SOARING. KEEP THRIVING. STAY POSTIVE. BE RELENTLESS. BE RESILIENT.

SOAR!

Notes

Notes

10

He is our Shepherd

Scripture: Psalm 23:1

The LORD is my Shepherd; I shall not want.

The LORD is my shepherd I shall not want. When we water our souls daily with these great promises our lives will blossom and bear spiritual fruits for the Kingdom of God. Oh Glory to God He is our shepherd, a shepherd takes the very best of his sheep. Aren't you rejoicing? Knowing that God is our shepherd and nothing will He withhold from us his sheep. We are protected there is no lack.

When we look in our cupboards, although sometimes the reality is it looks empty but we are still thanking God for His daily provision. He is able and faithful. Whatever the situation, we must decree and declare God's faithfulness in our lives, in the lives of our family and friends. As we continue to speak God's Word in and over our situations we will see His hand at work, we must believe and trust God.

Prayer: Our Father in Heaven, thank you for being our Shepherd, you protect, you provide and you guide. Thank you for daily provision in Jesus' Name Amen.

"All flower doesn't bloom at the same time."
-Ann Marie Bolton

Chapter Eleven

Under Spiritual Construction

Your foundation must be solid and the Creator who is the Architect is infusing all the right material to ensure a solid foundation. These are some of the components of a solid foundation: Spiritual steel, spiritual building blocks, spiritual cement and water which is necessary which represents the flowing of the anointing of the Holy Spirit and the prosperity of the saints.

After completion, your foundation is unshakeable you can withstand any hurricane, tsunami or storms that you may face on your journey. Obstacles and hurdles will now be viewed as spiritual strength. This topic is further dissected in this entire journey, the processing for your promise. You will be taken out of your comfort zone and will be purified for your intended purpose. This topic is an in depth discussion the processing for our Divine Purpose. God is at work on our behalf.

The promises of your life will come to pass but there is a process: during the purification process it is necessary to cultivate the right attitude or else you will be placed back in the fire for further formation. All of which will be outlined in the following pages on processing for your purpose. Perfect example: the children of Israel we all know that story very well.

The Israelites saw the many miracles but yet they walked by sight and not by faith and their unbelief displeased God and of such, failure to believe in God's word kept them from entering the Promised Land.

God is a promise Keeper, He never fail. He cannot fail. That's not His nature. He is an on time God. Whatever you are believing for trust God and it will come to fruition. Walk the walk and talk the talk with boldness and enthusiasm. On our journey, invest in equipping ourselves and others, that's how successful people think, not of themselves only but of others also.

You may be concerned about things you have done in the past, in the past, yes in the past: do not allow a negative past to define a positive future. You have a divine destiny, God has forgiven you that is his nature. He is a forgiving God, do not be so hard on yourself. The mind is a battlefield: detox the mind and think of positive things. Set yourselves free from mental slavery and look through your eyes of faith in every situation.

Notes

Notes

11

No Fear

Scripture: 2 Timothy 1:7

For God hath not given us the spirit of fear; but of power, and of love, and of a sound mind.

Fear cripples, it shatters dreams, it allows you to operate out of the will of God for your lives. I decree and declare as of today fear is cancelled and terminated in our lives. We give immediate notice to the enemy and its agents. Fear has no place in the heart of a believer. Fear as in the acronym, False Evidence Appear Real. Fear is not real it is a stumbling block, creating a road block in order for you not to achieve your God-given destiny and goals.

As of today, make it up in your minds NEVER to allow fear to paralyse you. Anytime fear would want to show up verbally, open your mouths and rebuke fear in the Name of Jesus. There's power in the Name of Jesus. God has NOT given us the spirit of fear, but of power and of love and a sound mind. Declare this scripture daily over your lives and watch the enemy flee. Fear is an Enemy and we will not give him a foothold and certainly would not be a stronghold.

Prayer: Our Father in Heaven, thank you for giving us a spirit of power and love and a sound mind in Jesus' Name Amen.

"Flowers look to the sun and so does the eagles."
-Ann Marie Bolton

Chapter Twelve

Your past is your stepping stone

Your past may be one that you do not want to remember but your past is now a stepping stone for success. It was necessary for the fulfilment of the promise. The past is what gives experience and maturity: now you are better able to assist someone who is going through something you had already gone through.

You can now relate to this situation which makes you more effective. Ultimately, through this experience or sometimes experiences, which is the most often case, it makes you into a better person. Mistakes are valuable lessons and must be embraced.

Problems and promises walk hand in hand: negative situation faced with the right attitude, gives a victorious and positive outcome. Being ignorant, of the fact that there will be challenges on the journey, sometimes if not most of the time, we block our own blessing.

Invest wisely your time. Conduct a personal inventory and the result will lead you to action.
-Ann Marie Bolton

We need to get out of our own way. Sounds very strange but this is true. There are so much unlocked potentials barred inside our minds because of fear or what people will say or may think. Wake up! If you do, or not do, learn this, people will always talk.

So do and let your success be noised abroad. My advice, in your success be humble and not arrogant. Work smart and reap great success. This is your time my brother. This is your time my sister, step out on centre stage. The promise must be fulfilled.

Whatever tactics, schemes, or plot the enemy has to try, to block or stop the promises of God in your life is cancelled now in Jesus' Amen. The enemy is defeated and he is powerless in Jesus' Name. Amen. Every mind blinded spirits are removed and broken in Jesus' Name Amen. The curse and the spell is broken in Jesus' Name. Amen. Hallelujah? Rejoice, rejoice, praise and worship your God because he is worthy.

You may have received a dream or vision and it is a promise from God and you keep on procrastinating, that is the enemy trying to intercept a divine appointment. You should have started your own business because you are an entrepreneur, write your book, pursue a new course of study, and the list goes on: but the enemy shows you every reason why you are going to fail and you believe the lie of the enemy and never activated the vision.

The irony of all of this is: how are you going to fail if you do not start? Get started in the name of Jesus, He will see you through to completion all you need to do is, start. Why wait?

The enemy can only try to stop the promise of God but he cannot. As in the case of Joseph, look what his own brothers did to him.

You intended to harm me, but God intended it for good to accomplish what is now being done, the saving of many souls.
Genesis 50:20(NIV)

In God's perfect timing and season the promise must come to pass. Everything that occurred on the journey, was just equipping and preparing you for the supernatural manifestation. There will also be some people who are hard to deal but thank God for them, they are your sandpaper people.

They are assisting in the processing and are a part of the fulfilment of the promise. You may have a very mean and unkind Manager but thank him or her for the help. While in the fire it may be difficult praise God but to praise God. Praise God in the fire and confuse the enemy: help is on the way.

He said, "Look! I see four men walking around in the fire, unbound and unharmed, and the fourth looks like a son of the gods". Daniel 3:26

The promise of God must come to pass, in due season and with due diligence. Sow good seeds and most importantly sow on good ground. Speak the positive and you will earn and receive positive results.

Our goals can only be reached through a vehicle of a plan, in which we must fervently believe, and upon which we must vigorously act. There is no other route to success. - Stephen A. Brenan

People of God let us pay attention to the prompting of the Holy Spirit for the promise to be fulfilled. We are no longer on our own agenda. We are on God's agenda and we are in God's perfect plan for our lives, let us live and operate accordingly. God's plan for your life is for you to have good success and nothing less: but you must believe that for yourself.

You must open your own mouth and speak the promises of God and rely, be confident and trust his promises only. Man will fail but God cannot fail. He is a faithful and merciful God. You must be believe. God is waiting on you to open your mouth to declare his promises over your life, for your life.

You will never be defeated, it may look like that in the natural but you are gaining in the spiritual. Your guardian angel is working on your behalf. God has given his angels charge to watch over us to ensure our safety enroute to the promise. Harness the power of belief and everything will fall into place.

Say to the Israelites, this is to be my sacred anointing oil for the generations to come. Do not pour it on anyone else's body and do not make any other oil using the same formula. It is sacred, and you are to consider it sacred. Exodus 30:31-32(NIV)

Notes

Notes

12

God Loves Us

Scripture: John 3:16

For God so loved the world that he gave his one and only Son, that whoever believes in him shall not perish but have eternal life.

As a parent of two sons, I give God thanks. God in His sovereignty gave His only Son, Our Lord Jesus Christ to die for us. Yes His only Son, what great love God has for you and me. All He requires is from us is that we love Him and appreciate Him for the sacrifice He made for us. If you are reading this devotional and you have not accepted Christ as your personal Lord and Saviour will you please give Him a chance in your life.

Let us not take it for granted but let's pause daily to thank God for His sacrificial love towards us. When He bore the scars to His hand, feet and side. When the crown He wore, was a crown of thorns it was for you and me. Oh Lord we thank you and we love you. You did it all for me. Now it is your time what will you give in exchange for your soul?

Prayer: Our Father in Heaven, come and make my heart your home. Thank you for sending your one and only son to die in our stead. We thank you in Jesus' Name Amen.

"Some flowers are tall while some are short but they all serve their purpose."
-Ann Marie Bolton

Part 2

My Prayer Garden

The Garden of Gethsemane
Matthew 26:36-46

God plants seeds of greatness in us, like a beautiful garden we nurture the seeds and watch them grow.
-Ann Marie Bolton

A FLORIST PRAYER

God prunes us the way florists prune their flowers
The florist watch and water the roses
The Florist nurture her flowers by talking to them
God wants us to be as attentive to Him,
the way we are attentive to our plants.
-By Ann Marie Bolton

My Prayer Garden is a journey of faith, favour and praise.

I was inspired to write this prayer journal because we sometimes find the time to speak to our plants and take the Creator for granted. We may all be able to attest to this truth. Plants cannot survive for long without water and sunlight. The very same is true for the spirit man, it cannot survive without the Word of God. Daily communion and fellowship, declaring the Word of God nurtures and refreshes our souls, making it into a luscious spiritual garden.

Speaking for myself, I also speak to my plants and would you believe me, these plants are the healthiest looking plants. I must acknowledge my sons Ricardo and Rhori who put up with me because plants were everywhere and are still everywhere. My sons know how much I love my plants and they sometimes say mom too many plants, get rid of some. That never happened. They played soccer and destroyed some of them and they knew for sure they would be in trouble with mommy because of my love for my plants.

It inspires me greatly to write my prayer garden because prayer means everything to me. My daily communion and devotion for the things of God are paramount in my life and will be for my journey here on earth. Come with me as we journey together in a wonderful prayer garden decorated with the most beautiful flowers of love and thanksgiving while building a meaningful relationship with the Creator.

We will take a stroll through the pages of the Bible,

we will explore some bouquet of adventurous verses and for sure decorated with prayers. Jesus Christ is referred to as the Lily in the valley and the Sweet Rose of Sharon. The Lily is beautiful and white in nature which represents purity. The Rose signifies beauty and is the most beautiful of all followers. The rose is found everywhere and in all countries. It is popular and loved by everyone. As we gaze on the Word through the eyes of a florist let us see the beauty in the Word and envelope ourselves with the leaves of the Bible. You will be glad you did.

I can assure you, your lives will be positively transformed and you will never be the same. Please journey with me.....

13

You Are Gifted

Scripture: 2 Timothy 1:6

For this reason I remind you to fan into flame the gift of God, which is in you through the laying of my hands.

Friend you were called to do great exploits under the anointing of the Holy Spirit. God has placed His anointing on you for a purpose. Being timid or afraid will block you from your God-given destiny.

Fan into flame the spiritual deposits, that God himself has laid His hands on you and trust you enough to anoint you and place it in you. Just in case you think you are not anointed seek for the anointing. The anointing gives power and allows you to operate in the supernatural gifting of God.

Fan into flame my brothers and sisters the spiritual gifts and let God have His way.

Prayer: Our Father in Heaven, thank you for choosing me and trusting to anoint me. Help dear Lord to fan into flame your gifts by using them to honour you and serve others in Jesus' Name Amen.

"The beautiful flowers get their light from the sun. They are well watered and fed by the Creator."
-Ann Marie Bolton

14

God Is Calling Young Men

Scripture: 1 John 2:14

I have written unto you, fathers, because ye have known Him that is from the beginning. I have written unto you, young men, because ye are strong, and the Word of God abideth in you, and ye have overcome the wicked one.

Young men as you water the flower garden with your mom or your wife, may God continue to shower you with His blessings. Watering your garden and plants reminds us how we should water the soil of our souls with the Word of God.

I can recall as a young married couple my husband always connect the hose to water my beautiful flower garden. He then connected a system like the rain to do the watering. That is how I loved my plants and watering my plants reminds me of how I should take the very same interest and more for the things of God.

God is the Creator, He created us all. Young men God has called you because you are strong. Be a good example and seek Christ and share Him with others.

Prayer: Our Father in Heaven, help our young men to be strong and courageous in Jesus' Name Amen.

"Flowers when planted proves to us that we have faith in God, because we expect them to grow."
-Ann Marie Bolton

15

God Is Always With Us

Scripture: Hebrews 13:5

Let your conversation be without covetousness; (and be) content with such as ye have: for he hath said, I will never leave thee, nor forsake thee.

God will never leave us or forsake us. He loves us so much that He sent His only Son Jesus Christ to die for us. Yes He gave His only Son Jesus Christ to to die for us. What conditional love. Thank you Lord.

I DECLARE God is going before me making crooked places straight. He has already lined up the right people, the right opportunities and solutions to problems. I haven't had no person, no sickness, no disappointment, can stop His plan. What He promised will come to pass. This is my declaration. –Joel Osteen

Whatever you are believing God to do with an attitude of faith God will ensure it come to pass. With every promise there must be a process, in order for it to be fulfilled into a purpose. When a promise is orchestrated by God it MUST come to fruition, perfect example, Joseph and his brothers. God was with Joseph and he obtained favour from God.

Joseph had a dream at a very young age, he was only seventeen (17) years old when he got this dream but God had his hand on him and he watched over Joseph and ensured the fulfilment of Joseph's dream.

Prayer: Our Father in Heaven, I thank you that you are with us, thank you for dreams and visions that you will see come to pass in Jesus' Name Amen.

"Your heart is like a flower open it and decorate the world." -Ann Marie Bolton

16

He is The Rose of Sharon

Scripture: Song of Solomon 2:1

I am the rose of Sharon, and the lily of the valleys.

In our prayer garden, Jesus is the Rose of Sharon, Christ expresses Himself in such elegant way. Making comparison to himself like that of the Rose of Sharon and the lily of the valley.

Roses are one the most beautiful flowers in one's garden and when we identify prayer as beautiful as roses what tapestry and beauty. Our souls are beautifully decorated with God's love and His grace. There is great ambiance in our prayer garden because God is with us.

May our souls be forever be decorated with God's grace, so our souls can be as fruitful and lush as a beautiful garden.

Let's Pray

Our Father, thank You that You are the beautiful Rose of Sharon and the lily in the valley. Thank you Lord for everything in Jesus' Name Amen.

"Cultivate your own garden and make yourself a bouquet. Celebrate yourself and encourage yourself."
-Ann Marie Bolton

Conclusion

"My mother taught me how to nurture and maintain a beautiful garden. She was my first role model and the sweetest and best mom. The way she cared for her plants they could be mistaken for human beings. I likened my mother to that of a pink rose. She taught me as a child to grow seeds of greatness with my words. My mother was the sweetest rose ever in the garden of my life. She grew love, compassion, knowledge, values and attitude and wisdom in her beautiful flowers garden."

-Ann Marie Bolton

Motivational Quotes

By Ann Marie Bolton

"Believe in yourself and invest in yourself"
-Ann Marie Bolton

Tap into untapped resources and transform your life and others positively.
-Ann Marie Bolton

Life without a plan is a wasted life.
-Ann Marie Bolton

Connect with people who will elevate you.
-Ann Marie Bolton

Spread joy and happiness into your darkest situation, with a positive attitude.
-Ann Marie Bolton

Sleepless and you will envision a bright future.
-Ann Marie Bolton

In Helping others you help yourself.
-Ann Marie Bolton

The family of God is never a broken.
-Ann Marie Bolton

Do not waste time with people who do not embrace your passion.
-Ann Marie Bolton

Betrayed but not bitter.
-Ann Marie Bolton

Single mothers are a gem.
-Ann Marie Bolton

Worship elevates a believer.
-Ann Marie Bolton

Unmask your potentials.
-Ann Marie Bolton

Purpose leads to self-actualization.
-Ann Marie Bolton

Release yourself, take the limits off.
-Ann Marie Bolton

People are depending on you to lead
them to greater success.
-Ann Marie Bolton

Wisdom is the building block to success.
-Ann Marie Bolton

What material is in the foundation of your life?
-Ann Marie Bolton

In releasing people you release yourself.
-Ann Marie Bolton

Spread a kind word daily.
-Ann Marie Bolton

How do you see you?
-Ann Marie Bolton

I am ambitious
I am strong
I am wise
I am caring
I am lovable
I am wealthy
I am healthy
I am blessed
I am trainable
I am forgiven
I am redeemed
I am anointed
I am a worshiper
-Ann Marie Bolton

Do good at all times.
-Ann Marie Bolton

You can make it.
-Ann Marie Bolton

Do not look back.
-Ann Marie Bolton

You are almost there, do not give up.
-Ann Marie Bolton

Chosen for greatness.
-Ann Marie Bolton

Build bridges in relationships.
-Ann Marie Bolton

Hold no grudge, forgive quickly.
-Ann Marie Bolton

Persistence, passion, perseverance and
purpose are the four P's of success.
-Ann Marie Bolton

Bad habits are easy to come by but hard to break.
-Ann Marie Bolton

Go on vacation in your mind and then make it a reality.
-Ann Marie Bolton

Decorate your mind like a beautiful bouquet.
-Ann Marie Bolton

What is in the garden of your mind?
-Ann Marie Bolton

Envelope yourself with love.
-Ann Marie Bolton

Throw out baggage out of life and walk freely.
-Ann Marie Bolton

Sleep is like a refresher course.
-Ann Marie Bolton

A healthy spirit is a contagious spirit.
-Ann Marie Bolton

CPSIA information can be obtained
at www.ICGtesting.com
Printed in the USA
BVHW030754090820
585781BV00013B/20/J

9 781984 583734